Houghton Mifflin

Daily Analogies

Level **3**

Caroline W. Ruesswick

Houghton Mifflin Company   Boston
Atlanta   Dallas   Geneva, Illinois   Palo Alto   Princeton

ISBN 0-8123-7252-2

Copyright © 1991
McDougal, Littell & Company
Box 1667, Evanston, Illinois 60204
All rights reserved. Printed in the United States of America
95 96 97 - CMC - 15 14 13 12 11 10 9 8

Introduction

Purpose
The purpose of the *Daily Analogies* program is to develop creative-thinking skills, to foster a diversity of problem-solving techniques, and to build reading skills through vocabulary enrichment. Because analogical thinking requires flexibility of thought and the application of a variety of verbal skills, many educators consider the ability to recognize analogies a strong indicator of academic success.

What is an Analogy?
An analogy is an expression of relationship. It is a proportional statement in which the relationship between two things is likened to the relationship between two others. For example, the analogy

> *Shoe* is to foot as *hat* is to *head*

states that a shoe is related to a foot in much the same way that a hat is related to a head: A shoe is worn on the foot, and a hat is worn on the head. In this case, the analogy is expressed verbally, but analogies can also be nonverbal, involving numbers or figures—for example,

> 4 is to 5 as 7 is to 8

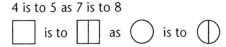

In any particular analogy, however, all terms must be of the same type—that is , all words, all numbers, or all figures.

Analogies are usually written with the symbols : ("is to") and : : ("as"). Thus,

> shoe : foot : : hat : head

is read "Shoe is to foot as hat is to head."

Program Design
The *Daily Analogies* program consists of nine teacher's manuals, one for each grade level from first through eighth and one for high school. The Level 1 manual contains thirty-one weeks of work; the manuals for the other levels contain thirty-six weeks of work each. The material for a week is printed on a single page of the manual and is divided into five daily lessons, each of which consists of a single analogy (in Level 1) or a pair of analogies (in the other levels).

The lessons are presented in a four-column format, with a representative day's lesson appearing as follows:

Day	Analogy	Possible Solution	Type
1	1. rectangle: _____ : : triangle : three 2. eyes : sight : : ears : _____	four hearing	characteristic agent/action

The first column indicates the recommended day for using the lesson. In the second column, "Analogy," is found the incomplete analogy or analogies that are to be written on the board that day. The third column, "Possible Solution," contains an example of a way in which each analogy might be completed. It is important to recognize, however, that in most cases there is more than one possible solution to an analogy. As long as a student can identify a reasonable relationship between the given terms of the analogy and can logically support his or her solution, that solution should be accepted.

In the last column, "Type," there is given a possible interpretation of the type of relationship exemplified by each verbal or numerical analogy. (There are no "Type" entries for pictorial analogies.) The analogy "shoe : foot : : hat : head," for example, is based on a relationship of *location*—the second term on each side tells where the item named by the corresponding first term is worn. The categories used in the program are based, for the most part, on those suggested by Johnson and Pearson:*

1. Object/function	broom : sweep : : knife : cut
2. Characteristic	ice cream : sweet : : pickle : sour
3. Part/whole	handle : cup : : knob : door
4. Whole/part	bird : claw : : dog : paw
5. Location	student : school : : sailor : ship
6. Action/object	run : track : : swim : pool
7. Agent/action or agent/object	teacher : pupil : : doctor : patient
8. Class or synonym	smell : sniff : : see : look
9. Familial	grandfather : father : : father : son
10. Grammatical	hear : heard : : see : saw
11. Temporal or sequential	first : third : : fifth : seventh
12. Antonym	smile : frown : : happy : sad

Johnson, Dale D., and P. David Pearson, *Teaching Reading Vocabulary* (New York: Holt, Rinehart and Winston, 1984).

The following two categories have also been used:

13. Degree	warm : hot : : cool : cold
14. Arithmetical	(1 + 2) : (5 − 2) : : (3 + 3) : (7 − 1)

The "Type" entries have been provided to help you guide students to a recognition of the basis of each analogy. Again, however, if a student discovers and justifies a type of relationship other than the one listed, his or her response should be accepted. Students need to be aware that there are a variety of ways in which words, ideas, and visual forms may be related. Such awareness will help them to recognize conceptual relationships in all areas of their studies.

The program begins in the sixth week of Level 1 with pictorial analogies, the solution of which demands visual discrimination, attention to detail, and identification of position and orientation. These analogies may be helpful in overcoming some students' confusion of shapes that are reversals or transpositions of each other (for example b and d, p and q, saw and was). The pictorial analogies presented in weeks 6–11 of Level 1 also incorporate the teaching of the names of colors and shapes. In week 12 of Level 1, verbal analogies are introduced. Thereafter, and throughout Levels 2–8, however, pictorial analogies continue to appear at the rate of two per week.

Halfway through Level 2, students begin to be exposed to analogies in which a term other than the last has been omitted. These serve to broaden students' approach to analogical thinking, since the relationships between their terms may be less readily apparent. In Level 3, "crossover" analogies are introduced—ones in which the first term is related to the third as the second is to the fourth, such as

air : water : : breathe : drink
two : three : : twins : triplets

Time sequences and arithmetical relationships also begin to be stressed in Level 3. Levels 4 and up contain analogies that involve the terminology of such content areas as math, the sciences, and social studies; prefixes and suffixes; and abbreviations.

Topics and Skills

The analogies presented in the program involve a diversity of important topics and skills. Among these are

General vocabulary	raise : increase : : _____ : decrease
Days of the week	Monday : Thursday : : Saturday : _____
Months	March : _____ : : November : March
Holidays	Halloween : October : : _____ : November
Time sequences	7:25 : 8:10 : : 9:15 : _____
Irregular past tenses	buy : bought : : throw : _____
Irregular plurals	child : children : : ox : _____
Abbreviations	illus. : illustration : : supt. : _____
Contractions	have not : haven't : : will not : _____
Prefixes and suffixes	-ful : full of : : _____ : without
Mathematics	(9 + 9) : (20 − 1) : : (_____) : (20 − 4)
Content area terms	cirrus : cloud : : chinook : _____

Teaching Procedure

Each day, write the appropriate lesson's incomplete analogies on the board, allowing the students to read them silently. (If you think that some students may be unfamiliar with certain of the words or with the symbols used in analogies, you may wish to read them aloud to the class.) After the students have had time to contemplate the analogies, ask volunteers to complete the analogies orally as you write their solutions on the board. *Be sure that students explain the reasoning that underlies their solutions.* Then lead a class discussion of the solutions. Remember, there are no "right" answers. Students are remarkably inventive and should be encouraged to discover as many relationships as they can, provided that they can justify their reasoning. Keep an open mind.

As you draw on the board the pictorial analogies presented in weeks 6-9 of Level 1, either color each figure the designated color or place a piece of paper of that color within the figure. In weeks 10 and 11, the figures should no longer be colored, but the color words should still be included.

At first, the students may have trouble conceptualizing the relationships expressed by analogies; and even when they have become adept at solving analogies, individual students will always be puzzled by particular problems. It is a good idea, therefore, to get students into the habit of creating sentences in which they focus on possible relationships between the given terms. For instance, when discussing the analogy

black : white : : night : _____

you might suggest that students say to themselves, "Black *is the opposite of* white just as night *is the opposite of* day." Similarly, to complete the analogy

pull : wagon : : paddle : _____

students might say to themselves, "You pull a wagon *to move it* just as you paddle a canoe *to move it.*"

Occasionally, the whole class may be stumped by a particular analogy, with the students perhaps being able to identify the relationship on which the analogy is based even though they cannot supply an appropriate term to complete it. In such cases, ask the class what kind of reference work (for example, an atlas, an encyclopedia, a dictionary, or a thesaurus) might contain the answer they are looking for. After students respond, have volunteers consult the suggested work or works to find a reasonable solution, and allow the volunteers to explain their solution to the rest of the class.

Time Management

Each daily lesson should require no more than five to ten minutes to complete and discuss. You may wish to conduct this activity at the beginning of the school day—perhaps allowing the students to ponder the analogies while you take attendance—so that it will establish a thinking environment for the rest of the day. It is important that you present the analogies daily, since providing the students with continual practice will build creative-thinking skills far better than, for example, asking them to deal with a week's worth of lessons in one twenty-five-minute session. Do not dwell on any one lesson—remember that these analogies are but one part of a total language-arts program.

Oral Emphasis

The emphasis in *Daily Analogies* is on the oral explanation of analogies—that is, on identifying and describing to others the relationships on which the solutions are based. If you wish to have students do their work on paper, have them copy the incomplete analogies from the board, perhaps in their journals, and then write their solutions. You should still, however, conduct an oral discussion of the various solutions, since such discussion will help develop the thinking skills of the students, particularly those who may have trouble recognizing the relationships expressed by the analogies.

Evaluation

For the convenience of teachers who wish to formally evaluate students' analogy-solving abilities, every level of *Daily Analogies* contains blackline masters of two tests—a Midyear Test, to be administered after week 18, and an End-of-Year Test, to be administered after week 36. Each test in Levels 1–3 contains ten problems; those in the other levels contain twenty problems each. These tests, which consist of incomplete analogies similar to those that the students have been solving each day in class, can be reproduced and distributed to the students as paper-and-pencil tests.

Daily Analogies

Day	Analogy	Possible Solution	Type
1	1. begin : start : : end : _____ 2. glad : happy : : mad : _____	finish angry	synonym synonym
2	1. before : after : : inside : _____ 2. (oval with cross) : (circle) : : (rectangle with 4 cells) : _____	outside (square)	antonym
3	1. moth : clothing : : termite : _____ 2. baseball : mitt : : boxing : _____	building gloves	agent/object object/function
4	1. tree : branch : : flower : _____ 2. (filled up triangle) : (open down triangle) : : (filled right triangle) : _____	petal (open left triangle)	whole/part
5	1. below : above : : far : _____ 2. shower : bathroom : : oven : _____	near kitchen	antonym location

WEEK 2

Day	Analogy	Possible Solution	Type
1	1. light : dark : : love : _____ 2. cow : calf : : lion : _____	hate cub	antonym familial
2	1. beginning : middle : : middle : _____ 2.	end 	sequential
3	1. scissors : cut : : broom : _____ 2. lamp : light : : furnace : _____	sweep heat	object/function object/function
4	1. full : empty : : more : _____ 2.	less 	antonym
5	1. window : pane : : eyeglasses : _____ 2. man : boy : : woman : _____	lens girl	whole/part degree

Daily Analogies

Day	Analogy	Possible Solution	Type
1	1. 7:15 : 7:30 : : 9:15 : _____ 2. teacher : student : : coach : _____	9:30 player	temporal/sequential agent/object
2	1. many : few : : more : _____ 2. ◨ : ◆ :: ◨ : _____	less ◆	antonym
3	1. think : thought : : throw : _____ 2. Christmas : December : : Halloween : _____	threw October	grammatical temporal
4	1. swim : swam : : draw : _____ 2. ⬡ : ◯ :: ⬡ : _____	drew ◯	grammatical
5	1. house : roof : : head : _____ 2. United States : country : : Texas : _____	hair state	whole/part class

WEEK 4

Day	Analogy	Possible Solution	Type
1	1. potato : vegetable : : grape : _____ 2. few : many : : always : _____	fruit never	class antonym
2	1. sister : brother : : niece : _____ 2. ◆ : ■ : : ◆ : _____	nephew ■	familial
3	1. wall : brick : : skeleton : _____ 2. horse : barn : : car : _____	bone garage	whole/part location
4	1. hospital : doctor : : school : _____ 2. ● : ■ : : ◈ : _____	teacher ◆	location
5	1. 10:45 : 11:15 : : 1:45 : _____ 2. book : read : : record : _____	2:15 listen	temporal/sequential action/object

Day	Analogy	Possible Solution	Type
1	1. thread : needle : : key : _____ 2. Thanksgiving : November : : Christmas : _____	lock December	object/function temporal
2	1. hungry : eat : : tired : _____ 2.	sleep 	action/object
3	1. rain : cool : : snow : _____ 2. backward : forward : : away from : _____	cold toward	characteristic antonym
4	1. ocean : wet : : desert : _____ 2.	dry 	characteristic
5	1. engine : car : : light bulb : _____ 2. paint : brush : : draw : _____	lamp pencil	part/whole object/function

WEEK 6

Day	Analogy	Possible Solution	Type
1	1. yesterday : today : : today : _____	tomorrow	temporal/sequential
	2. ant : insect : : robin : _____	bird	class
2	1. bread : wheat : : paper : _____	wood	object/function
	2.		
3	1. poodle : dog : : oak : _____	tree	class
	2. handle : suitcase : : knob : _____	door	part/whole
4	1. paint : wall : : dye : _____	cloth	action/object
	2.		
5	1. send : receive : : throw : _____	catch	antonym
	2. ball : round : : box : _____	square	characteristic

Daily Analogies

Level 3
WEEK 7

Day	Analogy	Possible Solution	Type
1	1. baby : weak : : gorilla : _____ 2. pig : farm : : tiger : _____	strong jungle	characteristic location
2	1. mouse : cat : : thief : _____ 2. ⬛(rectangle w/ diagonal) : ▱(parallelogram w/ diagonal) : : ▭(rectangle w/ diagonal) : _____	police officer ▱(parallelogram w/ diagonal)	agent/object
3	1. bicycle : tricycle : : two : _____ 2. perfume : nose : : music : _____	three ears	characteristic agent/object
4	1. sun : Earth : : Earth : _____ 2. ⧨ : ∧∧∧ : : ↑ : _____	moon →	agent/object
5	1. sleeping bag : tent : : bed : _____ 2. mural : painting : : lullaby : _____	house song	location class

WEEK 8

Day	Analogy	Possible Solution	Type
1	1. train : station : : airplane : _____ ✓ 2. mirror : reflect : : knife : _____	airport cut	location object/function
2	1. wind : sailboat : : _____ : car 2. : : : : _____	gas 	agent/object
3	1. can : metal : : towel : _____ 2. peach : lemon : : sweet : _____	cloth sour	characteristic characteristic
4	1. sunset : red : : banana : _____ 2. : : : : _____	yellow 	characteristic
5	1. seaweed : _____ : : cactus : desert 2. heat : boil : : cold : _____	ocean freeze	location agent/action

Day	Analogy	Possible Solution	Type
1	1. 1 : 5 : : 3 : _____ 2. hammer : _____ : : hoe : gardener	7 carpenter	sequential agent/object
2	1. steak : steer : : bacon : _____ 2.	pig 	object/function
3	1. foot : big toe : : _____ : thumb 2. hawk : bird : : yellow : _____	hand color	whole/part class
4	1. stegosaurus : _____ : : gorilla : ape 2.	dinosaur 	class
5	1. pillow : soft : : _____ : hard 2. _____ : sheep : : cowboy : cattle	rock shepherd	characteristic agent/object

WEEK 10

Day	Analogy	Possible Solution	Type
1	1. rectangle : square : : oval : _____	circle	characteristic
	2. tadpole : frog : : _____ : butterfly	caterpillar	familial
2	1. catcher : baseball : : goalie : _____	soccer	agent/action
	2. : : : : _____		
3	1. neigh : horse : : chirp : _____	bird	agent/action
	2. picture : see : : music : _____	hear	action/object
4	1. wall : poster : : _____ : stamp	envelope	location
	2. : : : : _____		
5	1. pig : snout : : elephant : _____	trunk	whole/part
	2. one : penny : : _____ : dime	ten	characteristic

Daily Analogies

Day	Analogy	Possible Solution	Type
1	1. twelve : sixteen : : fourteen : _____	eighteen	sequential
	2. _____ : coal : : blue : sky	black	characteristic
2	1. peas : spinach : : apple : _____	pear	class
	2. : : : : _____		
3	1. frog : _____ : : duck : waddle	hop	agent/action
	2. market : _____ : : forest : woods	store	synonym
4	1. cow : calf : : deer : _____	fawn	familial
	2. U : ∩ : : T : _____	⊥	
5	1. ruler : inches : : _____ : pounds	scale	object/function
	2. body : skin : : banana : _____	peel	characteristic

WEEK 12

Day	Analogy	Possible Solution	Type
1	1. remember : forget : : _____ : lose	find	antonym
	2. fingers : _____ : : ears : two	ten	characteristic
2	1. largest : smallest : : _____ : shortest	tallest	antonym
	2.		
3	1. bread : butter : : salad : _____	dressing	location
	2. _____ : water : : suitcase : clothes	bucket	object/function
4	1. leg : knee : : arm : _____	elbow	whole/part
	2.		
5	1. horse : hay : : rabbit : _____	carrot	agent/object
	2. clouds : _____ : : grass : ground	sky	location

Day	Analogy	Possible Solution	Type
1	1. wet : dry : : _____ : hot 2. flowers : garden : : fruit : _____	cold orchard	antonym location
2	1. trainer : dog : : teach : _____ 2.	learn 	agent/action
3	1. _____ : huge : : dwarf : small 2. flower : flour : : not : _____	giant knot	characteristic grammatical
4	1. dog : leash : : balloon : _____ 2.	string 	object/function
5	1. friend : _____ : : wise : foolish 2. lady : ladies : : sheep : _____	enemy sheep	antonym grammatical

WEEK 14

Day	Analogy	Possible Solution	Type
1	1. Halloween : witch : : _____ : bunny	Easter	characteristic
	2. has : _____ : : had : hadn't	hasn't	grammatical
2	1. fish : scales : : crab : _____	shell	characteristic
	2. ⟨△△⟩ : [△△△] : : ⟨▽▽⟩ : _____	[▽▽▽]	
3	1. paste : glue : : _____ : pupil	student	synonym
	2. frog : jump : : horse : _____	gallop	agent/action
4	1. penny : coin : : dollar : _____	bill	class
	2. ⊟ : ▣ : : ⊡ : _____	⬛	
5	1. ten : twenty : : 10 : _____	20	arithmetical
	2. should : shouldn't : : will : _____	won't	grammatical

Day	Analogy	Possible Solution	Type
1	1. hammer : _____ : : shovel : dirt	nail	agent/object
	2. small : smaller : : smaller : _____	smallest	degree
2	1. film : camera : : ink : _____	pen	object/function
	2. ⬆⬆ : ▼▼ : : ⬇⬇ : _____	△△	
3	1. _____ : children : : baby : babies	child	grammatical
	2. trees : forest : : _____ : lake	water	location
4	1. everywhere : nowhere : : everyone : _____	no one	antonym
	2. (●○ ●) : (○● ○) : : [■ ▯ ■] : _____	[▯ ■ ▯]	
5	1. tent : camping : : _____ : sailing	boat	object/function
	2. city : cities : : spy : _____	spies	grammatical

WEEK 16

Day	Analogy	Possible Solution	Type
1	1. judge : _____ : : teacher : classroom 2. _____ : spoon : : salad : fork	courtroom soup	location agent/object
2	1. book : page : : harp : _____ 2. [symbol] : [symbol] : : [symbol] : _____	string [symbol]	whole/part
3	1. love : hate : : _____ : cry 2. lollipop : _____ : : apple : bite	laugh lick	antonym action/object
4	1. carpenter : board : : plumber : _____ 2. [symbol] : [symbol] : : [symbol] : _____	pipe [symbol]	agent/object
5	1. mean : nasty : : _____ : gentle 2. beginning : end : : start : _____	kind stop	synonym antonym

Day	Analogy	Possible Solution	Type
1	1. store : _____ : : restaurant : eating 2. mammal : camel : : _____ : peach	shopping fruit	location class
2	1. whisper : soft : : scream : _____ 2. △(○) : (○●●) : : △(●) : _____	loud (●●●)	characteristic
3	1. snow : shovel : : leaves : _____ 2. soldier : army : : sailor : _____	rake navy	agent/object part/whole
4	1. candy : _____ : : pretzels : salty 2. ◇(●○) : □(●○) : : □(●○) : _____	sweet ◇(○●)	characteristic
5	1. car : gas : : person : _____ 2. silk : sandpaper : : _____ : rough	food smooth	agent/object characteristic

WEEK 18

Day	Analogy	Possible Solution	Type
1	1. airplane : wings : : car : _____	wheels	part/whole
	2. sail : sale : : see : _____	sea	grammatical
2	1. run : swim : : track : _____	pool	location
	2. : : : : _____		
3	1. minute : clock : : _____ : thermometer	degree	object/function
	2. tear : torn : : _____ : broken	break	grammatical
4	1. seven : fourteen : : three : _____	six	arithmetical
	2. : : : : _____		
5	1. president : country : : governor : _____	state	agent/object
	2. bury : buried : : cry : _____	cried	grammatical

A reproducible Midyear Test is included at the back of this book.

Day	Analogy	Possible Solution	Type
1	1. rectangle : _____ : : triangle : three	four	characteristic
	2. eyes : sight : : ears : _____	hearing	agent/action
2	1. thin : thinner : : thinner : _____	thinnest	degree
	2. : : : : _____		
3	1. ski : skate : : _____ : ice	snow	location
	2. blood : _____ : : water : pipe	vein	object/function
4	1. ride : rode : : sit : _____	sat	grammatical
	2. : : : : _____		
5	1. catch : throw : : _____ : pull	push	antonym
	2. blind : _____ : : deaf : hear	see	characteristic

WEEK 20

Day	Analogy	Possible Solution	Type
1	1. inches : feet : : ounces : _____ 2. _____ : library : : money : bank	pounds books	part/whole location
2	1. thief : steal : : customer : _____ 2. **43** : **34** : : _____ : **21**	buy **12**	agent/action
3	1. baby : _____ : : eagle : soar 2. foot : feet : : _____ : hooves	crawl hoof	agent/action grammatical
4	1. Monday : Thursday : : _____ : Tuesday 2.	Saturday 	temporal/sequential
5	1. spend : _____ : : dig : dug 2. talk : speak : : jump : _____	spent leap	grammatical synonym

Day	Analogy	Possible Solution	Type
1	1. weak : _____ : : dark : light 2. order : command : : _____ : request	strong ask	antonym synonym
2	1. train : airplane : : station : _____ 2.	airport 	location
3	1. small : tiny : : large : _____ 2. movie : actor : : ballet : _____	huge dancer	degree agent/object
4	1. daisy : flower : : canary : _____ 2.	bird 	class
5	1. _____ : coal : : well : water 2. hill : mountain : : stream : _____	mine river	location degree

Day	Analogy	Possible Solution	Type
1	1. restaurant : _____ : : playground : play	eat	location
	2. close : _____ : : distant : far	near	synonym
2	1. city : mayor : : state : _____	governor	agent/object
	2. (triangle figures)	(triangle figure)	
3	1. alike : different : : strength : _____	weakness	antonym
	2. dog : bird : : paw : _____	claw	characteristic
4	1. noun : word : : vowel : _____	letter	class
	2. (shape figures)	(shape figure)	
5	1. arms : shoulders : : _____ : hips	legs	location
	2. apple : pie : : lettuce : _____	salad	object/function

Day	Analogy	Possible Solution	Type
1	1. _____ : sunset : : morning : evening	sunrise	temporal/sequential
	2. Pacific : _____ : : Sahara : desert	ocean	class
2	1. telescope : far : : microscope : _____	small	object/function
	2. : _____ : : :		
3	1. glasses : reading : : crutches : _____	walking	object/function
	2. cows : herd : : lions : _____	pride	part/whole
4	1. _____ : crops : : gardener : flowers	farmer	agent/object
	2. : : : : _____		
5	1. pig : squeal : : _____ : roar	lion	agent/action
	2. lamb : _____ : : kitten : cat	sheep	familial

WEEK 24

Day	Analogy	Possible Solution	Type
1	1. same : opposite : : synonym : _____	antonym	antonym
	2. plus : add : : _____ : subtract	minus	synonym
2	1. belt : buckle : : jacket : _____	zipper	whole/part
	2. : : : _____ :		
3	1. top : bottom : : _____ : under	over	antonym
	2. fifty : _____ : : twenty : twentieth	fiftieth	grammatical
4	1. violin : bow : : guitar : _____	pick	object/function
	2. : : : : _____		
5	1. heart : blood : : stomach : _____	food	agent/object
	2. halt : stop : : aid : _____	help	synonym

Day	Analogy	Possible Solution	Type
1	1. octopus : eight : : insect : _____ 2. car : garage : : _____ : hangar	six airplane	characteristic location
2	1. mother : _____ : : aunt : niece 2. _____ : ◣◥ : : ▷ : ◄►	daughter △	familial
3	1. sail : sale : : blew : _____ 2. lightning : thunder : : fire : _____	blue smoke	grammatical agent/object
4	1. tall : height : : _____ : distance 2. ▣ : ▢ : : ◈ : _____	long ◈	characteristic
5	1. liquid : solid : : _____ : ice 2. two : twins : : three : _____	water triplets	characteristic characteristic

WEEK 26

Day	Analogy	Possible Solution	Type
1	1. duck : feathers : : tuna : _____ 2. beginning : _____ : : end : suffix	scales prefix	characteristic location
2	1. United States : North America : : France : _____ 2. : : : : _____	Europe 	location
3	1. worst : best : : _____ : most 2. dictionary : definition : : atlas : _____	least map	antonym part/whole
4	1. gills : fish : : _____ : cat 2. : : : : _____	lungs 	part/whole
5	1. soccer : _____ : : English : language 2. Whole House : _____ : : palace : king	sport president	class location

Daily Analogies

Day	Analogy	Possible Solution	Type
1	1. bear : cub : : goat : _____ 2. airplane : train : : _____ : engineer	kid pilot	familial agent/object
2	1. north : northwest : : south : _____ 2.	southeast 	sequential
3	1. monkey : tree : : hippopotamus : _____ 2. poem : _____ : : painting : artist	river poet	location agent/object
4	1. boulder : stone : : stone : _____ 2.	pebble 	degree
5	1. dust : dry : : _____ : wet 2. Chicago : Illinois : : city : _____	mud state	characteristic class

WEEK 28

Day	Analogy	Possible Solution	Type
1	1. messy : _____ : : boring : dull	sloppy	synonym
	2. ax : blade : : comb : _____	teeth	whole/part
2	1. door : wall : : _____ : fence	gate	location
	2.		
3	1. once : single : : twice : _____	double	characteristic
	2. necklace : bead : : chain : _____	link	whole/part
4	1. clumsy : graceful : : gloomy : _____	cheerful	antonym
	2.		
5	1. tailor : cloth : : butcher : _____	meat	agent/object
	2. depart : _____ : : go : come	arrive	antonym

Day	Analogy	Possible Solution	Type
1	1. _____ : calendar : : day : clock 2. Monday : Sunday : : Friday : _____	year Thursday	object/function temporal/sequential
2	1. pepper : spice : : pecan : _____ 2.	nut 	class
3	1. 7:25 : 7:45 : : 9:10 : _____ 2. length : weight : : _____ : ounces	9:30 inches	temporal/sequential object/function
4	1. penny : dollar : : centimeter : _____ 2.	meter 	part/whole
5	1. (5 + 2) : _____ : : (9 + 6) : (10 + 5) 2. mare : foal : : mother : _____	any sum = to 7 child	arithmetical familial

WEEK 30

Day	Analogy	Possible Solution	Type
1	1. win : _____ : : whisper : yell	lose	antonym
	2. _____ : wrist : : sleeve : cuff	arm	whole/part
2	1. I : I'm : : he : _____	he's	grammatical
	2. ◯ : ▢ : : ◎ : _____	▣	
3	1. comb : _____ : : shine : shoes	hair	action/object
	2. (4 + 3) : (6 + 1) : : _____ : (3 + 3)	any sum = to 6	arithmetical
4	1. bicycle : wheel : : sled : _____	runner	whole/part
	2. ◈ : ◹ : : _____ : ◹	◇	
5	1. soap : clean : : _____ : dirty	mud	object/function
	2. actor : _____ : : musician : concert	play	agent/object

Daily Analogies

Day	Analogy	Possible Solution	Type
1	1. submarine : ocean : : satellite : _____ 2. tepee : igloo : : skins : _____	space snow	location characteristic
2	1. (6 + 4) : (5 + 5) : : (8 + 7) : _____ 2. ⬭ : △ :: ◻ : _____	any sum = to 15 △◻	arithmetical
3	1. dog : paw : : fish : _____ 2. lioness : cub : : _____ : piglet	fin sow	part/whole familial
4	1. glass : break : : paper : _____ 2. ⬭ : ◯ :: ⬭ : _____	tear ◯	action/object
5	1. 6:03 : 6:42 : : 10:10 : _____ 2. lake : water : : _____ : trees	10:49 forest	temporal/sequential location

WEEK 32

Day	Analogy	Possible Solution	Type
1	1. sandwich : bread : : pie : _____ 2. bread : flour : : butter : _____	crust cream	whole/part object/function
2	1. light : reflection : : _____ : echo 2.	sound 	agent/object
3	1. (7 + 5) : (15 − 3) : : _____ : (18 − 3) 2. two : three : : double : _____	any sum = to 15 triple	arithmetical characteristic
4	1. barber : _____ : : tailor : cloth 2.	hair 	agent/object
5	1. lend : borrow : : _____ : catch 2. (3 + 2) : (_____) : : (11 + 3) : (21 − 7)	throw any difference = to 5	antonym arithmetical

Day	Analogy	Possible Solution	Type
1	1. cold : warm : : freeze : _____ 2. first : last : : most : _____	thaw least	antonym antonym
2	1. finger : ring : : wrist : _____ 2. [diagram] : _____ : : [diagram] : [diagram]	bracelet [diagram]	location
3	1. ore : metal : : wheat : _____ 2. inside : outside : : _____ : outer	flour inner	object/function antonym
4	1. (9 – 6) : (2 + 1) : : (_____) : (3 + 10) 2. [diagram] : [diagram] : : [diagram] : _____	any difference = to 13 [diagram]	arithmetical
5	1. hour : our : : _____ : their 2. knapsack : backpack : : branches : _____	there limbs	grammatical synonym

WEEK 34

Day	Analogy	Possible Solution	Type
1	1. cat : kitten : : _____ : fawn 2. alive : dead : : _____ : worst	deer best	familial antonym
2	1. yell : whisper : : wild : _____ 2.	tame 	antonym
3	1. (6 + 5) : (14 − 3) : : (7 + 6) : _____ 2. kettle : soup : : _____ : pancakes	any difference = to 13 griddle	arithmetical object/function
4	1. peanut butter : sticky : : cracker : _____ 2.	crunchy 	characteristic
5	1. run : race : : eat : _____ 2. rope : knot : : _____ : bow	meal ribbon	action/object object/function

Day	Analogy	Possible Solution	Type
1	1. bear : den : : bee : _____ 2. (8 + 8) : (7 + 7) : : (_____) : (8 + 6)	hive any sum = to 16	location arithmetical
2	1. eggs : scramble : : potatoes : _____ 2.	mash 	action/object
3	1. palm : finger : : _____ : limb 2. gnaw : chew : : tremble : _____	trunk shake	location synonym
4	1. surgeon : operation : : _____ : trial 2.	judge 	agent/action
5	1. palace : _____ : : yacht : boat 2. canoe : paddle : : bicycle : _____	house pedal	class action/object

WEEK 36

Day	Analogy	Possible Solution	Type
1	1. daisy : rose : : plum : _____ 2. oboe : woodwind : : violin : _____	apple string	class class
2	1. bottom : top : : cellar : _____ 2.	attic 	location
3	1. hungry : starving : : _____ : exhausted 2. (11 + 4) : (21 – 6) : : (_____) : (17 – 7)	tired any sum = to 10	degree arithmetical
4	1. classroom : teacher : : school : _____ 2.	principal 	location
5	1. cold : shiver : : hot : _____ 2. _____ : sentence : : sentence : word	sweat paragraph	action/object whole/part

A reproducible End-of-Year Test is included on the following pages.

Name _____ Date _____

1. hand : finger : : flower : _____

2. teacher : _____ : : coach : player

3. painter : _____ : : carpenter : hammer

4. : : : : _____

5. brain : head : : heart : _____

6. picture : see : : music : _____

7. largest : _____ : : tallest : shortest

8. has : hasn't : : _____ : hadn't

9. love : hate : : laugh : _____

10. mask : _____ : : hat : head

1. _____

2. _____

3. _____

4. _____

5. _____

6. _____

7. _____

8. _____

9. _____

10. _____

MIDYEAR TEST

ANSWER KEY

1. petal

2. student

3. brush

4.

5. chest

6. hear

7. smallest

8. had

9. cry

10. face

Daily Analogies

Name _____ Date _____

1. blind : see : : deaf : _____   1. _____

2. rose : flower : : bluejay : _____   2. _____

3. duck : _____ : : lion : roar   3. _____

4. two : _____ : : three : triplets   4. _____

5. symphony : _____ : : novel : author   5. _____

6. Monday : Wednesday : : _____ : Friday   6. _____

7. : : : : _____   7. _____

8. classroom : teacher : : courtroom : _____   8. _____

9. frogs : tadpole : : _____ : caterpillar   9. _____

10. _____ : snow : : drop : rain   10. _____

END-OF-YEAR TEST

ANSWER KEY

1. hear

2. bird

3. quack

4. twins

5. composer

6. Wednesday

7.

8. judge

9. butterfly

10. flake